I0755938

FINISHING LINE PRESS
www.finishinglinepress.com

HALLWAYS

poems by

Allen Strous

Finishing Line Press
Georgetown, Kentucky

HALLWAYS

ISBN 979-8-89990-432-5 First Edition

ACKNOWLEDGMENTS

ArLiJo: "Another"
Blue Unicorn: "Clock and Mirror," "Coal," "Long Moment," "Visual"
Bohemian Renaissance: "Afternoon"
Caesura (Poetry Center San Jose): "Narrative Consciousness"
The Cortland Review: "Hallways," "Lamplight," "Reading," "The Gap," "Earthed"
Illya's Honey: "Damascene," "Promise," "Story"
Oracle (Brewton-Parker College): "Mrs. Reichelderfer's Grape Hyacinths"
Off the Coast: "Addictions"
Referential Magazine: "Beatitudes"
The Rockford Review: "New Holland"
Rockhurst Review: "Springs," "Summer Afternoons at Thirteen"
Trajectory: "Deictic"
"Vacant" first appeared in *Watching the Perseids: The Backwaters Press Twentieth Anniversary Anthology,* ed. Cat Dixon, Michael Catherwood (Omaha: The Backwaters Press, 2017)

Publisher: Leah Huete de Maines
Editor: Christen Kincaid
Cover Art: "Jackson Township Centralized Schools," Pickaway County, Ohio
Author Photo: Brad Laxton/Laxton Photography LLC
Cover Design: Elizabeth Maines McCleavy

Order online: www.finishinglinepress.com
also available on amazon.com

Author inquiries and mail orders:
Finishing Line Press
PO Box 1626
Georgetown, Kentucky 40324
USA

Contents

Hallways

The machine minder
not in the machine yet—
mind remaining
gray space,
gray wadding of the headache,

waste space,
saved by inefficiency, past it,
the gray glide of the hallway,

the fire escape from my sixth-grade classroom,
World War I-time building,
the stairwell, down two floors,

grandeur of
mope—
            The little box thinks of grandeur—
the stairs' rise, turns,
space of pure geometry, featureless,
the walls' grayed white no-color.
Had the plaster ever been painted—
past such attentions—

and the windows—
one into a first-floor "cloakroom,"
two panes of frosted wire glass
for a little light struggling onto that landing near the bottom,
how nearly pointless
and *there*   it is

and up, up,
the long window high on the wall at the top—
let it stay long and drafty with just sky,

window   nature
other—

nature
not so definite as usual, not details crowding in,

just space
allowing,
just walking outdoors

other   allowing.
I am here and there is more
of

I   am here,
all vague.

Someone's music, talk could crowd in and crowd me out,
someone's cheery elementary school.
With waste space, I stand a better chance.

Addictions

The dark only a little haggarded by my moving through it
in the first minutes of waking,
bringing some sleep along,
my eyes adjusted, half-open, half-shut,
half-knowledge,
routine and whole.
There is only me   only these steps of mine, these paths
burrowed through the still-dark,
no abysses around.

I make these ragged cycles—
the cup, the pill, the rocking chair
rocking toward the warm core
here already,
my treadle working nothing
more and more.

Clock and Mirror

It is and it isn't.
In the still moment of the room

these are not still,
they are still,
      little motion, over and over
hardens.

The room
still
soft
as feathers or soot,
better than this glitter,
its untruth
becoming true, gray, in the wearing on and on,
a little.

Cool,
composed,
conscious,
the clock's many moments
fall into a well,
dark riding, indefinite.

As for the mirror's brightness
doubling
conscious of the moment
which gets beyond it,
and the room in the mirror
extending beyond the edges.

Lamplight

Yellow and brown
low intensity
usual

the homemade lamps for an electric bulb
or the kerosene lamps converted,
with a bulb now

ineffective   reminiscent of the kerosene

little light
casting darknesses

the usual way   this nightscape   roomscape
here, here

from there   it stretches,
so given

no question, anymore,
change unthinkable—
change this   glared away
a nowhere   homelessness

The books turn yellow and brown, dim down,
the newspaper,
the usual
looked at intently
each classified a little hearth
and what hearths, further
in each glowing coal

if not much glow,
just the usual,
these little boxes

familiar block downtown
round and round, again
and the new, the more, it contains.

Another

Two rooms,
one
and
an other

and passing between them

secret passage   secret rooms
as if in the fold of a curtain,
in the shadow there
more shadow, shadows   all vague
what this would be, how this would fit
runs on   the fast jet slow in the sky, the slow of it   that real

while, from one room into
those photographs,
points of view, from each window, each angle,
each point   seeing from each point,
contained, complete,
this many
each   other

—seeing each, for a moment, other

Coal

Closing in,
closing down,
compression
though it burns,
burns this way

burning darkness
of the miner's heft,
shedding darkness,
dark winter weather

of the houses.

The sharpness of the stench of burning
tears no holes,
closing in, closing down

the fiery mountain ranges in the stove,
no heights—down, in,
bright blind,
blackness in the red.

Damascene

Time loosens the cement and asbestos siding shingles, a little
still here, but the start of ramshackle
run,
this live stream—
in the streaming, the straight lines not in nature
into nature,
out of plumb
in the slant rain of time,

that rain into them, time into them,
not bright shiny no-time—the look of them runs,
a watered silk, water running,
happening, the way the window's frostwork happens, grows.

The industrial products grow mysterious with time,
no longer   made like that,
time rained in,
no longer   changed now
with lengthening time

in them, lengthening them,
not found in any store
where nothing is,
that mass shiny flow.

New Holland

Hard to believe,
but there on the flatland, outcrop—
hard to believe
the geography textbook's products of

but the routines of the houses are just as solid.
The solids of the square, squarish houses are undeniable.
Even the bank's letterhead, a conscious modernity
of 1960 achieving it

an outcrop, a wart,
that independent

for the grocery store, hardware store
to supply
the necessities, their own,
not conduits of other or of wonder
blanking out this place.

Reading

A small dead tree on the slope of the hill
hung in the sky,
all the carve of branches, bark.
Darkness, stated.
A drawing, emphatic,
and the space it hangs in, emphatic as framed space,
absolute, no sense of littleness with that frame.

Like a drawing, it is nothing
really,
and this drawing means nothing—
still it means,
the merely dead tree with its background of air,
a puzzle
with its sure look,
emptied symbol, meaningless, meaning.

Narrative Consciousness

After the university library
    the cool light on the pages,
    the light in the black and white of the pages
    moving

driving home, out of the town—
on the way
the little car
all the night
enclosing

mind still moving, escaped,
daytext
expansive, the lit landscape, no discernible final edges.

Rust

Blood rusts, from its freshness,
a deliverance.

Rust stains from the lightning-rod cables on the roof,
so old they are timeless

standing in blue blue sky
that never had time,
a stainless steel
that walls an endless hole
though wallless here
and not devouring,
not quite.

Long Moment

Fall
in the window,
the maple and October sky,
cathedral gold leaf and blue
burst—
what has grown
clean, pared.

It will not stiffen to its frame.
It will not break the frame
this moment
on and on
and changing
and changing into evening

and what music for it, what words,
a sog of too much, for this moment,
and of only a little, frozen moment,
what then—

consciousness
on,
with its unconsciousnesses, through the day

maybe words after all then, a running on and on, flickering,
words and the spaces between words, the stops, running on,
the low relief there.

Promise

The closet wallpaper
maybe in the whole room,
red roses browning on brown, browning—
the vague sentimental absolute
and even more   that brown,
what the coming rain contains,
age spot, meaning there was more,

all the dimensions, distances in the chintzy out-of-date
in that upstairs bedroom of the cottage we weren't supposed to be in,
but one of the big kids had to use the bathroom
    all yellow and brown, of its time, of age
at the park, site of our mothers' ladies' club picnic

someone knew how to get in, said it was all right.
The big kids know,
with kindly a few of us five-year-olds in tow
of their glamor.

They knew so much, looked so good, so sure,
so *there*, as much as the grown-ups, without the haggard draining
  started.

    Though I grew, I was never there, never have been,

never in that round wading pool
that we passed and passed that day,
where I wanted to go,
know the water, that other,
so little of it in my inland childhood.
There would have been no water-heaviness—
in it would be flight,
that feeling, that easy, without my fear of heights,
just seeing myself in some more brilliant air,
being brilliant in it

in fields of roses,
a delirium of roses,
not the florist's vases
but what is in the fold of a cloud,
out
where—
more than out,
not so definite
but more tremendous.

The wallpaper still blooms in a closet somewhere.

Springs

I.

In April
when there is color,
not dimmed with summer glare yet,
and not too cold color,
the enamel not, only, repelling,

in the new greens of the new leaves coming,
deep in the right morning light, holding
      plummet of leaves
so deep
      through, into their depth and their darkness,
essence of fluid there
all feeling

only feeling
this life
repelling, too pure to be lived.

II.

Not the realized brightness
but the cloudy, troubled

black earth of the air—
edge,
silver, of this screen, all the carved wisps,
then essence of blue, too dark for blue, containing,
pregnant of, not one—
how many, what—
and I felt that

in me,
the coming,
knowing, unknowing
of what all was to come.

The Gap

They talked too much of happiness,
of too much.

Take that word *happiness—*
turn it over and over, smooth stone in the hand.
It is there, there may be happiness, but

the stone breaks and this opens up

a crack
in the summer evening where the daylilies burned last
what burned through

layers of evening,
the going, the coming, glimmering
between
beyond

in the light then   and into the light
the country that opens up there,
the cleanness of it come back to where I was,

no finicky fineness
but the fineness in the dandelion's gold
      through

It was this gap
that filled,
set me in motion,

something in the head,
something in the air,
there   air

I'm searching,
reaching, reaching

always wanting a hole.

Mrs. Reichelderfer's Grape Hyacinths

riotous flowers, wild scrollwork
put in order
that billows out and out
on the wallpaper, on printed cottons,

in, among the white abstractions,
square structures of the farmstead,
squares of the farm, fields—
pattern of the checkerboard, more or less
billowing out,

the house the barn the sheds, precise pieces—
Does the old woman keep them precise,
no scatter of clutter of children now,
clutter, so abundant,
what life more abundant—

the old woman's life,
amid a plain glory of cleanliness,
the life that this life lets:

free tree
the huge maple, one limb a blacksmith's arm crooked out
of order, out over the yard fence, the road, blessing the road,
and tangled outside the fence,
daffodils, even grape hyacinths
running into the pasture. She planted them.

Vacant

the old house will be saved,
empty for years

now just a sign, signs,
the realtor's signs, changing
how people come and go

so not again—
made new,
the rest of the farm to be gone
in newness of houses

but how will the emptiness be saved

the dead dark brown of the door,
the brown, still browning wall past the opened door,
in and out the gauntness of the upstairs windows,
the black glass skying,
centrifugal of skies.

But the new life will be so small,
simple, single,
only quiver, excitement,
leaving no room,
the insistence of holiday decorations

where will be the wind, gray, winding of the old house

The window fills
with curtains,
with fill,
filled,
blinded.

Visual

Past the angle of the building's entry, a blank wall,
the concrete extending in front of it.
On a fine fall afternoon, light and shadow
too big and simple for a play of light and shadow.

The entry's raised flowerbed extended too,
chrysanthemums now,
hardly meant to be seen either,
but an eye in this,
if not seeing, giving the fine light.

Earthed

How old is the sunlight, arrived here—
how new, ever new, here—
neither, nothing to do with me
—the too-ordinary summer day, clogged humid,
sick photograph,
dull light-writing—the utilitarian note left on the table,
the ordinary half-real

but the afternoon the sunlight was real,
into the new grave, onto a corner of the old vault
accidentally unearthed—still coated with dirt
over the well-preserved metal's phony elegance
now with age and earth
new enough—here again, and just here.
A massiveness, mass, holds,
the dirt comfortable on the gardener's fingers,
a smile of crooked teeth,
awkward, natural, something turned up in the garden.

Afternoon

We want to be day,
onward
          not onward, here
the progress of the light,
the clock's ticking.

There is such a thing as afternoon

and I

look at some very 60's houses,
thinking of life that looks like the advertising,
life that is the advertising,
beautiful, supposedly,
all to be seen,

thinking,
in the beautiful room
the daydream self is beautiful—

all the junk kids waste their allowances on, for this—

time wasted making the junk for a paycheck,
what doing
or what—

while I find I've gone on,
afternoon after
                    afternoon

the light on the walls
become the weight of the light on the walls,
the history of

still the light on the walls

past doing or saying,
finally, something,
some light of
my own afternoon.

Story

Oh I could tell you stories
    after mention of the cousin who broke his arm
    in the dare jump fall
    from the bluff into the river

the girl's voice a story,
its lilt narrative,
fitting together   how could it break
its story escapes, goes on

past the afternoon moment
a story
without incident
fit together   our bubble of fluorescent light, the study hall,

the light outside the windows going on, a story,
the monitor not paying attention for the moment,
so the girl goes on
like the afternoon light,
the monitor's withdrawal   dark   what—a story

going on
past the time that devours narratives
or has swallowed these
whole, still,
long after this remembered moment.

Summer Afternoons at Thirteen

The afternoons free, with no obligation,
like the sun through the windows—
multiple windows, multiple slants of light
caught at different angles, in glimpses at room doors,
down on my grandmother's old copy of Tennyson, on the Christmas
 cactus, on a chaste kitchen stool just to hold it,
all these turnings, down on the farm.
I could turn outside on a summer vacation afternoon—call it aimless—
under all that sky, sheer sweep, still multitudinous—
knowing of all those angles, points of view,
knowing of the precision of each,
the sunny afternoon in a cloud of knowing
vaguely—knowing there was more
horizonally, under, in the sky, but sure of this scape's
each and each and each,
and knowing some of the small points, smally, pointedly.
I thought this pointillism was seeing, still with some kindly vagueness,
 like God.

Beatitudes

I.

Praise,
a usual sigh,
for the sink, the electric stove,
making so smooth and still and ordinary.
Making a cup of instant coffee, I find myself in this household round
of a few steps in the kitchen.
They have painted the coffee-making, folding clothes beautiful.
This is not beautiful.
It does not run so far.
But finding myself here, congruent,
a few motions congruent with the task—
everything fitting,
if, like the linoleum, a list of instructions,
a formica shine, only
a little more,
a gray space of myself,
gray winter afternoon.

II.

Alone in the chore a minute,
alone in the room of the chore,
I find there is room, a room,
waiting here for the kettle to boil in a minute
and I find I am here,
not much,
pilot light,
so much a thing in its place
        —though the flame draws together far sources, their places
    known, and here too—
but this little light, simple,
gray flame.

III.

In the silent afternoon house
all day, every day I can,
that nothing
        the winter afternoon light, no burst of it,
        so steady, steadily vast
I and this—
familiar, faded out
is
walking in the light,
so light

the light, the sky at the top of the hill
I see from the foot of the hill

into the light

the light in

the figure on the plate border,
right and shining.

Deictic

Holding the snapshot/held by the snapshot
of my grandmother and my father, a toddler,
in an unknown backyard
maybe—
but she never owned a pair of white shoes, my father says,
a maybe store-bought print dress, so very patterned, patterned like
    that—
not even sure of this
another one

and why should a photo,
a handful of photos, dimly known, matter,
when things and things of the stores don't matter, the people
making, buying and selling don't

things in their thingness

all the rooms of bombed cities

....

not the rooms of bombed cities
that once—

an eddy of fallen leaves
so many   so many leaves, so many drifts of them,
one, becoming

    But there   of many, one

and making pattern of its patternlessness, making a place

quiet
close my eyes,
darkness
point   this one

the clutter on the table, the table under the window
    the

the eye digs a hole, a burrow,
its back to this wall in front of it, seeing this

this,
not one more.

Allen Strous is the author of *Tired* (The Backwaters Press). His poetry chapbook *Of This Ground* is part of the four-author collection *The Fifth Voice* (Toadlily Press). His poems have appeared in various journals, including *The Ohio Review* and *The Cortland Review*, and more recently *Blue Unicorn, Freshwater,* and *ArLiJo*. He has received Pushcart Prize nominations, and individual artist grants for poetry from the Ohio Arts Council.

www.ingramcontent.com/pod-product-compliance
Lightning Source LLC
LaVergne TN
LVHW090541110826
845146LV00003B/1206

* 9 7 9 8 8 9 9 9 0 4 3 2 5 *